THE REAL OLD WEST

Images of a Frontier

THE REAL OLD WEST

IMAGES OF A FRONTIER
Photographs by Frank Matsura

BY JOANN ROE

Introduction by Murray Morgan

Douglas & McIntyre   Vancouver   1981

FIRST EDITION

10 9 8 7 6 5 4 3 2 1

Douglas & McIntyre Ltd.
1615 Venables Street
Vancouver, British Columbia

Canadian Cataloguing in Publication Data

Matsura, Frank.
   The real Old West
   ISBN 0-88894-340-7

   1. Matsura, Frank. 2. Photography, Artistic.
3. Frontier and pioneer life — Washington
(State) — Omak — Pictorial works. I. Roe,
JoAnn, 1926-   II. Title.
TR653.M38   779'.092'4   C81-091348-8

Book design: Sally Bryer Mennell
Composition: Graphics West/Typeline, Seattle
Printing and binding: North Central Publishing Company, St. Paul

Printed and bound in the United States of America

Preface

Who was this man Matsura? Why did a fastidious Japanese man of apparent culture, rumored to be well educated, come from his homeland to work as a cook's helper in a backwoods town three hundred miles from Seattle? Who sent him money periodically and why?

One can speculate: He left Japan because he was a younger son in a family where the eldest gained the advantage. He had an unhappy love affair. He was a fugitive. But we don't know. Why didn't he go home to Japan when he became ill? Did he know he had tuberculosis in 1901? Did he come to the high, dry Okanogan country to try to recover?

A few people who remember him from their childhood days in Conconully and Okanogan assert, nearly seventy years after his death, that he was in the newspaper business in Japan. Others believe he had been a pantomime artist attached to the Japanese armed forces, that such entertainers were part of the military. (My Japanese researcher says that the latter is inconsistent with Matsura's apparent social level.) Newspaper accounts from Okanogan papers and written reminiscences shed little light on Matsura's thirty-nine years of life.

What is known is that Frank Matsura, the man, endeared himself to the rough-hewn pioneers, homesteaders, miners, and Indians of the Okanogan country. He became their brother. The *Okanogan Record* said after his death that he surely did not have an enemy in the world.

After nine months of intensive research, detective work that has led from Okanogan to Seattle, California, Denver, Sitka, Alaska, and Japan, we still have no answers—just a continuing mystery. Only one fact is circumstantially proven. In 1901, a Sakae Matsuura filled out a passport application in Japan, giving his destination as Tacoma-Seattle, his place of residence as Tokyo, at an address that no longer exists. Newspaper accounts from Okanogan County indicate that Matsura arrived in Conconully in 1903, after having lived in Seattle and traveled to Alaska. Two pieces of mail discovered among Matsura's effects, both from a woman named Noriko in Japan, are addressed in Japanese characters to Sakae and to Mr. S. Matsura. Matsura originally signed his photographs *Frank S. Matsuura*. This strong evidence indicates that Sakae and Frank were the same person. Noriko sympathized with Frank about the loss of a camera that the government gave him. The Japanese government? Why? Despite ongoing research in Japan, we have no definite answers.

Among the fascinating leads that have been pursued, all inconclusively, are:

Matsura may have sailed from Tokyo to Seattle on the *Riojun Maru,* a ship of the Nippon Yusen Line, a subsidiary company of Mitsubishi. A photo by Matsura of the ship was found among his negatives. The ship's records were destroyed in World War II.

Among Matsura's photos was one taken of a clipping from an undetermined newspaper that discusses the drowning of a Mr. Toda aboard a ship belonging to Nippon Yusen, Toda's employer. The clipping shows that Toda once taught English in a Kamamoto City High School in Kyushu Prefecture. Review of a list of the school's graduates does not uncover any Matsuura. However, there is a Matsura (not Matsuura) family in Kyushu Prefecture, so rich and powerful and famous nationally, that there is a Matsura museum in Hirato. There was a Sakae among family members. Nothing has been found, however, to connect Frank S. Matsura with this family.

What we do know is that Matsura photographed with consummate skill a period of transition in the American-Canadian West, a time when the cultures of homesteaders and Indians overlapped and mingled. Because of its cloistered location, with a towering mountain range to the west that inhibited intercourse with the urban centers of Seattle and Vancouver, the Okanogan country developed its own sociological and economic ideas. While Matsura may have come as a spectator of frontier life, bringing his camera to record it, he stayed to become a part of its history.

When Matsura died suddenly, his photographs, mostly on glass plates, went unnoticed for forty-one years. Having stored Matsura's effects after his death, Judge William Compton Brown, his friend, opened the boxes of photographic materials briefly in 1954 with the intention of cataloging them. But he did not do so. Sometime thereafter Brown gave certain of his own legal papers and research materials about Indian treaties to the archives at Washington State University, Pullman, Washington. Included with these papers was a part of the Matsura photographic collection.

Upon Brown's death in 1963, most of his property and effects went to Eva Wilson, who had taken care of him for several years. One day in 1964, Wilson telephoned Judge Joseph Wicks, Brown's friend and successor on the bench, and asked him about three boxes containing pieces of heavy glass in the garage—what were they, what should she do with them? Fortunately, Wicks remembered that Brown had retained a part of Matsura's collection—the best part, as it turned out—and asked Wilson to turn them over to the Okanogan County Historical Society. This small group of volunteer historians had no building, only a garage and orchard warehouse, to which the glass plates were removed.

When the society scrounged up sufficient funds to build a small museum at Okanogan in 1975, it rediscovered the Matsura collection among its other artifacts. Bruce Wilson, then publisher of the *Omak Chronicle* and a member of the Historical Society, selected some of Matsura's pictures to be enlarged for display in the museum. The *Chronicle* offered to store the valuable collection at its relatively fireproof offices, and since then it has had custody of the glass plates and negatives.

In 1974, while searching for illustrations of early Okanogan events, I obtained a few Matsura prints from the Okanogan County Historical Society for a book, *The North Cascadians* (Madrona Publishers, 1980). At that time I filed a mental note to return and delve into the mysterious Mr. Matsura's life more thoroughly. It was 1980 before I had time to do any sleuthing. The more I saw of his photographs, the more I heard about the man himself, the greater was my conviction that here was an undiscovered photographer of major importance. After seeing some of Matsura's prints and learning about Matsura, Madrona Publishers of Seattle and Douglas & McIntyre of Vancouver, B.C. enthusiastically agreed to publish the book internationally.

For help in the search for Matsura's past, a person to whom I owe great thanks is Thomas Kaase, Head of Reference Services, East Asia Library, University of Washington, who examined all the obscure lists and records known only to such a professional. They might have revealed, but did not, something about Matsura's Seattle life.

I appreciate the research assistance of Masahiko Shima, Tateyama City, Chiba Prefec-

6

ture, Japan, who was a student in 1981 at Western Washington University, Bellingham, Washington, and virtually an adopted member of our family. He translated Japanese materials and secured the help of his father, Kazuhiro Shima, in Japan. The latter made several trips to Tokyo to investigate leads, and enlisted the help of the Japan Photographers Association in Tokyo. The association reported that there was a famous photographer in Nagoya in about 1900 named Matsura, but there is nothing to link Frank S. Matsura with Nagoya. Back home in Japan during the summer of 1981, Masahiko continued his research and also contacted NHK, Nihon-Hoso-Kyokai, the Japanese Public Broadcasting Association. I appreciate the help, too, of Arata Hayashi of Osaka, who is also with NHK.

Thank you, Bill Hosokawa, columnist for the *Pacific Citizen,* a Los Angeles newspaper with largely Japanese-American readership, for writing about Matsura in an attempt to ferret out information.

I appreciate the cordial help of organizations in Seattle, which polled their most elderly members in a futile attempt to learn anything about Frank S. Matsura, or Sakae Matsuura — The Japanese American Citizens League, the Japan America Society of Seattle, Inc., the Japanese Baptist Church and its pastor, Rev. Paul M. Nagano.

For sharing personal reminiscences with me and in identifying situations and people in Matsura's photographs, special thanks go to pioneer Dora Storhow Meeker, who was extremely helpful. I also appreciate the help of Addie Mitchell, Moses George, Dorothy Mitchell, Lillian Kaufman, Howard Lockwood, Bill Roberts, the late Sen. Robert French, Alice Irey, Judge Joseph Wicks, Ada LeMaster, Susanne Manuel, Margaret Gorr, Ruth Murray, Don Jaquish, Blanche McSwane, Fred Baines, Bernard Kaufman, Rose Cox, Robert Gibson, and Carl Cleveland. I acknowledge with special thanks the help of Julianne Cecilia Timentwa in identifying photos of Indian people. Personal knowledge of early cowboys was furnished by Warren Dickson, and of grain farming by Ed McLean. My appreciation goes to Terry Abraham, Washington State University Archives, for his cooperation. A special thanks to Charles Goodyear of the Okanogan County Historical Society, who spent hours in the museum with me while I perused old newspapers. Thanks to Dennis Anderson, Northwest Collection, University of Washington; to Jeanne Coberly, Seattle Public Library; to Margaret Ziegler, Linda Hodge, Gail Helgoe, Jane Lawry and Bruce Radtke of the Bellingham Public Library reference staff. To my husband, Ernie Burkhart, goes my gratitude for his support and my appreciation for his own fascination with the Matsura saga.

A very special thanks to John E. Andrist, a talented photographer and member of the Okanogan County Historical Society, who made all but a few of the prints from the Matsura glass plates. It was a difficult and demanding job, involving work with fragile plates, some almost eighty years old. John became so engrossed in the task that he found himself talking out loud in the darkroom to Frank Matsura.

JOANN ROE

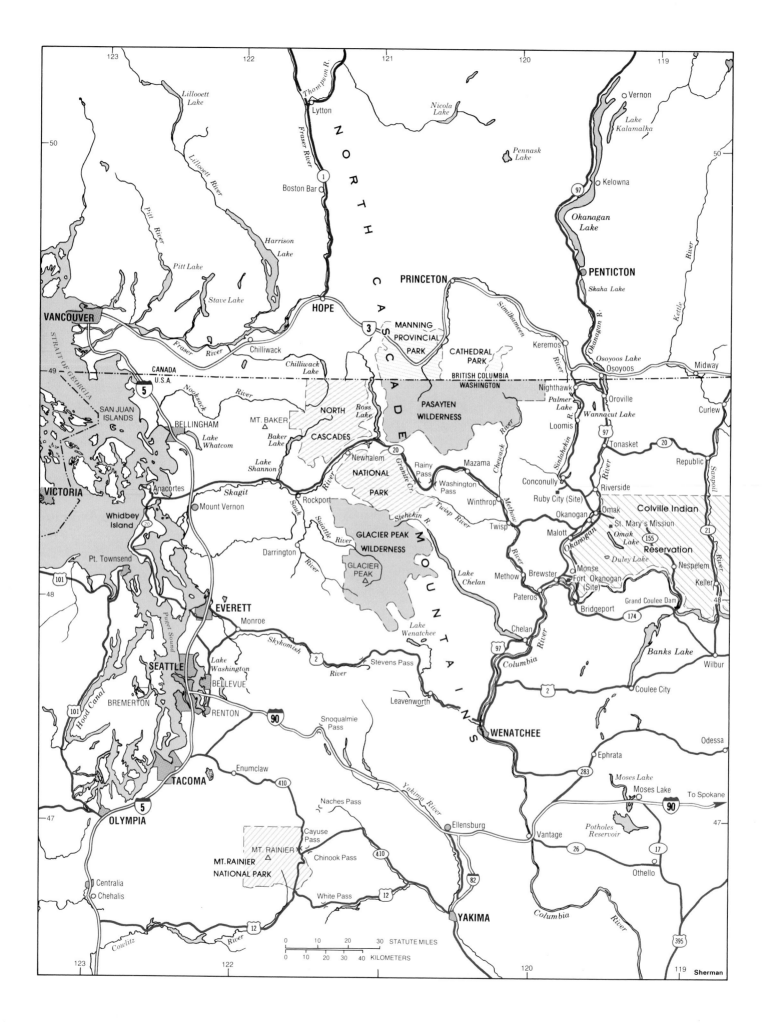

Introduction

MURRAY MORGAN

The settlements of Omak and Okanogan were younger than Frank Matsura was when the twenty-nine-year-old Japanese came with his camera and glass plates in 1903 to capture images of the last flowering of westward pioneer life in America.

For nearly half a century after the first white men saw the valley of the Okanogan in 1811, it was regarded not as a place to settle but as a pathway to somewhere else: down from the north to the Great Columbia Plain or up from the south to the mineral-rich mountains of the Kamloops and Cariboo in today's British Columbia.

Not until H. F. "Okanogan" Smith, a disappointed forty-niner, passed through the valley on his way to the Cariboo gold fields, then returned in 1860 to build a log cabin on the eastern shore of Lake Osoyoos, did anyone settle in the valley. And not until a minor mining excitement broke out in the Okanogan itself in the late 1880s was there significant American immigration.

David Thompson, the admirable map-maker and advance man for the British-owned North West Company, had been the first white man to hear of the Okanogan River. On his pioneering descent of the Columbia in 1811, Thompson camped among the Nespelem Indians on July 5. His hosts told him of "the high woody mountains of the Oachenawga River" just downstream, and offered "to dance for your good voyage and preservation." It rained hard the next day, though, and Thompson failed to see the mouth of the Okanogan as his canoe swept past it.

To David Stuart, a former Nor'wester then working for John Jacob Astor's Pacific Fur Company, went the distinction of being the first white man to find the Okanogan and ascend it the following September. Stuart and four companions, assigned to open an interior trading post, paddled and sailed a small dugout up the Columbia from the recently established Fort Astoria.

The juncture of the rivers looked promising to Stuart. The surrounding land was open, covered with bunch grass. Hummingbirds danced among the wildflowers. The hills to the west, dark with pine, offered promise of beaver. The Indians were friendly and had many horses. There were salmon in both rivers. The Astorians knocked together from driftwood a rude shelter, twenty by eighteen feet, and gave it the imposing name of Fort Okanogan. Stuart assigned Alexander Ross, a twenty-eight-year-old Scot who had abandoned school-teaching for the fur trade, to look after the post while the rest of the party explored the valley to the north. For the next six months, Ross and his little dog Weasel constituted the entire garrison.

The mountains humped higher and the pine trees stood taller and closer together as the Stuart party pushed up the meandering Okanogan. At the forty-ninth parallel, the present U.S.-Canadian border, they reached the long, shallow lakes the Indians described as *sooyos* —narrow. (A visiting Irishman is credited with adding a Celtic prefix and naming Lake Osoyoos.) The Astorians followed the river north to its source in Lake Okanagan (Canadian spelling), then pursued a small tributary until it trickled out in the mountains. Caching their dugout, they worked westward over a gentle range and found themselves on a branch of the Thompson River. Unexpectedly early snows forced them to winter among the friendly Shuswap Indians.

In the spring of 1812, Stuart's group returned to Fort Okanogan. The lonely Ross was delighted to have someone hear his tales about whiling away the winter by swapping £35 worth of trade goods for 1,552 beaver skins and miscellaneous other pelts worth, he estimated, £2,250 in China. Fort Okanogan, in spite of millions of mosquitoes and scores of rattlesnakes, seemed a great place.

That summer, after reinforcements arrived from Astoria, Ross retraced Stuart's trip upstream. He found the Okanogan Indians to be "by no means ferocious or cruel, either in looks, habits or disposition; but... on the contrary, rather an easy, mild and agreeable people." His heart agreed with his judgment, and he married an Okanogan girl.

When Ross reached the Thompson, the Shuswaps were so eager to trade that "one morning before breakfast I obtained 110 beavers for leaf-tobacco, at the rate of five leaves per skin, and at last, when I had but one yard of white cotton remaining, one of the chiefs gave me twenty prime beaver skins for it."

Despite the promising interior trade, the American venture on the Columbia did not prosper. Because of British naval superiority in the War of 1812, the Astorians felt obliged to sell out to the North West Company, which controlled the trade on the Columbia and its tributaries until 1821 when it, in turn, was absorbed by the Hudson's Bay Company.

Under the new proprietorship, Fort Okanogan and its namesake river became major links in the Pacific Northwest communication system. Trade goods shipped around Cape Horn from Britain to the Columbia usually arrived at Fort Vancouver in March. They were divided into ninety-pound packs ("pieces") and transported up the Columbia by canoes or eight-oared rowboats known as York boats.

The goods destined for New Caledonia, as the British Columbia interior was then called, were unloaded at Okanogan and transferred to pack horses. The trip up the Okanogan and across the mountains to Fort Alexandria on the Fraser usually took two weeks. The pieces were again loaded into canoes and sent on to Fort St. James, and from there they were sent to the outlying posts by horse, sled, canoe, or backpack. The return trip with the season's fur take from Fort St. James usually started early in May, and the furs reached Fort Vancouver in mid-June, to be loaded onto the supply ship, which returned to England by way of China.

For a quarter of a century the pack trains made their seasonal trips along the Okanogan. Father Demers, the first Catholic missionary in the area, described the passage as "slow and wearisome."

> Each morning's preparations [he wrote] are not finished until nine or ten o'clock. Horses let out haphazard during the night and scattered in every direction must be rounded up. After long delays you at last find everything ready, and the neighing of horses, the shouts of the engagés, the oaths jerked out by impatience, the disputes, the orders of the leaders form a hullabaloo by which scrupulous ears are not always flattered. At last, after having eaten on the grass a repast of dried salmon, the horses are loaded, and at ten o'clock you are on your way. The march is extremely slow and filled with incidents more or less disagreeable. There is a feverish atmosphere, an oppressive sun, a choking dust, a hill to climb, a ravine to cross. Halts are made only for camping, that is to say in the idiom of the country, one only hitches up once; and the day's travel ends in three or four hours.

The Okanogan trail lost importance when the Hudson's Bay Company found a new route for the brigade along the Similkameen and Coquille rivers to Hope, British Columbia, on the Fraser. The company abandoned Fort Okanogan after the Treaty of 1846 established the boundary along the forty-ninth parallel, which bisected the Okanogan Valley at Osoyoos. For a decade the valley below the line was left to the Indians. Then rumors and reports of gold around Fort Colville and on the Thompson and Fraser rivers started a stampede north.

Some gold-hungry Yankees followed the former Hudson's Bay Company trail to the diggings in British Columbia. Many soon found themselves hungry for things more important than gold. Ranchers who had been running cattle on the Great Columbia Plain met some of the need for food by driving herds up the Okanogan. This proved profitable, although some steers were lost when clouds of mosquitoes drove them to stampede over cliffs.

The bitter winter of 1860 destroyed most of the cattle on the Columbia Plain, and the price of beef rose dramatically. Ben Snipes gambled on buying more than a thousand head in the Willamette Valley at prices ranging from $6 to $16 a head, and driving them 600 miles to Barkerville in the Cariboo, where, he had been told, the half-dollar was the smallest coin used and three fried eggs cost $2. Snipes sold his critters for an average of $100 apiece and rode nervously back to the states with $100,000 in gold dust in his saddlebags and a reputation for being the "Cattle King of Oregon."

Canadian customs records show 22,256 head of cattle entering British Columbia by way of the Okanogan between 1859 and 1870, the peak years being from 1862 to 1866. The gold excitement was over by 1868, but it left as a legacy an extensive cattle industry in the grassland interior south of the border. It also left H.F. Smith on the bank of Lake Osoyoos.

Smith had hunted gold from California to the Cariboo, but in 1860 he stopped roaming and built a cabin on the eastern shore of Lake Osoyoos. The valley's first settler, he became its first representative to the territorial legislature. To get to the 1865 session, Smith had to go north into British Columbia, cross the mountains to Fort Langley, and proceed by steamer down the Fraser, Georgia Strait, and Puget Sound to Olympia. At Hope, on his return trip, be bought 1,200 seedling apple trees and some peach trees and took them by snowshoe and dogsled across the mountains to his homestead. The orchard he established on the sunny riverbank prospered. A few of his trees are still bearing, and today there are nearly two million apple trees in the Okanogan valley.

In the 1870s the growing agricultural potential of eastern Washington led to the redrawing of the boundaries of Indian lands established twenty years earlier. The object was to open more land to white settlement. In 1872 the Colville lands were created by executive order. Nestled in a cup formed by the bend of the Columbia and the south-flowing Okanogan, the Colville lands meant that much of the Okanogan valley was closed to white settlement until Smith, using his status as a pioneer and legislator, managed to get land opened first for mineral claims, then for settlement.

Almost immediately there were reports of minerals. A rush started that brought to the Okanogan daily stagecoach service, claims disputes, gunfights, an avalanche of mining stock, and an abundance of disappointment. The Okanogan mountains did hold some gold, some silver, and lots of epsom salt, but most of what was mined was undiluted country rock. Seldom did so many work so hard, so long, in hope of getting rich without working. More money was paid in than panned out during the rush, but by the time the last dream of bonanza had died at the turn of the century, Okanogan County (created by the legislature in 1888) had enough population to count.

It was still a backwater. Sternwheelers paddled eighty miles up the Columbia from

Wenatchee to Brewster, near the site of old Fort Okanogan; when the river was in flood, they could get all the way up to Riverside. But there was not railroad service until 1906, when James J. Hill ran a line from Spokane up into British Columbia, then back across the border to Oroville on Lake Osoyoos. Not until 1915 was there a direct rail connection with Wenatchee.

With the decline of prospecting, fruit-growing and ranching regained importance as the prime activities. Dr. Joseph Pogue, in 1888, had managed to lead water from Salmon Creek along gravity-flow ditches behind Omak and Okanogan. In 1902 a government-sponsored irrigation project was started, one of the first in the nation. The system was completed in 1910, and the first large crop was harvested in 1915.

Some orchardists and farmers set up small sawmills on their spreads. A mill usually consisted of a circular saw run by a steam engine, and a movable carriage to shove the log against the blade. The carriage might be powered by a steam engine, water wheel, horse, or the farmer's family. There was no formal logging. Most sawing was done for a fee. The mill owner cut logs hauled in by the customer and accepted his payment in boards. Not until 1921 when the Biles-Colman Company was formed at Omak to saw logs from the Colville reservation was there a true industrial mill.

Phelps and Wadleigh, cattlemen from Yakima, established a cattle station near Loomis in 1877. Though an estimated 8,000 of the 10,500 head in the Okanogan Valley died in the severe winter of 1879, the herds recovered quickly. Even after rail service began across the Cascades from Yakima to Tacoma in 1888, cattlemen found it profitable to drive herds through Snoqualmie Pass to market in Seattle. Beef can transport itself to market, but the going is slow. "You can't crowd cattle on the trail," one cowboy recalled, "but if you're driving them through Republic, you've got to get through that town before school lets out. There's nothing like kids to stampede a bunch of cattle."

The towns were not without amenities. Republic, hidden in the folds of the Okanogan highlands, had an opera house. Molson claimed the best hotel, the Tonasket, where rooms in the attic cost fifty cents a night, those on all other floors seventy-five cents, and meals thirty-five cents. Every town boasted of "one of the longest bars north of San Francisco and east of Portland."

By 1900, there was even telephone service. One hundred forty miles of line radiated from the central switchboard at Loomis (named for the town storekeeper) to clusters of settlers in the communities that now bear the names of Conconully (Okanogan for "beautiful land of bunch grass flats"), Oroville ("Gold Town"), Molson (for J. W. Molson, a Canadian promoter who never visited it), Brewster (for John Bruster, who home-steaded the site), Chesaw (for Chee Saw, a Chinese prospector who married a local Indian after the Cariboo rush), Malott (for W. G. Malott, an early settler), Golden (for a false hope), and Riverside.

Cows and cowboys, kids and one-room schools, steamboats round the bend, rail-roads in the offing, and telephone lines looping across the brown hills—such were the symbols of life in the Okanogan Valley in 1903 when Frank Matsura arrived from Japan to look with the eyes of a stranger on an America that would soon cease to exist.

Frank Matsura

...And they embalmed him and he was put in a coffin in Egypt.

Genesis 50:26

An appropriate text for the June 1913 funeral of the Japanese man who lay in his casket in Okanogan, Washington, a very long way from his home in Japan. Like Joseph, the biblical Israelite in Egypt, thirty-nine-year-old Frank Matsura was alone in a foreign land. No relative came to mourn him, no messages of sorrow came from abroad. The curt instructions of the Japanese consul in Tacoma had been, "bury him where he is."

Yet Frank S. Matsura was far from friendless. His funeral was held in the town's large auditorium because the mourners could not crowd into the church. More than three hundred people came to pay their respects—both whites and Indians, the Northwest people among whom he had chosen to make his home and seek his fortune. He left a legacy of photographs of the Okanogan country, taken between 1903 and 1913—pictures of unusual quality and historical importance that are a record of life on one of North America's last frontiers.

The Okanogan country, sloping eastward from Washington's towering North Cascades Mountains and the Coast Range in Canada, spilled from the ragged foothills carved by the Methow and Similkameen river systems down into the fertile valleys of the Okanogan and Columbia rivers. East of the rivers the land rose abruptly into arid mesas and brown, rolling rangelands interspersed with pine forests. Far north of the international border the Okanogan River started as an outlet for Lake Okanagan, winding southward through Lake Osoyoos to its rendezvous with the Columbia near Brewster.

It was a bountiful land with abundant salmon and trout in the rivers, camas bulbs and berries for the taking, plenty of deer and bear to provide pelts for clothing and tepees, vast grasslands for horses. Several bands of Indians—Okanogan, Colville, San Poil, Chelan, Moses, Kartar, Methow— all of a similar lineage, the Salish, lived in relative harmony in the Okanogan. Occasionally a trading party walked across the North Cascades to trade with coastal Indians for shells, much prized for jewelry.

Only seventeen years before Frank S. Matsura arrived in the Okanogan country, stepping off the stage at Conconully in 1903, this wild country had become a frontier—a confrontation beginning when settlers entered the Okanogan in significant numbers to mingle with the Indians and vie with them for land. These changes began in 1886, when the Moses Reservation was opened for homesteading and gold was discovered in the North Cascades and near the Canadian-American border.

Settled by the miners and merchants who followed the ever-swirling rumors of rich gold, silver, and copper finds in boom years that had passed, Conconully struggled to survive. It still clung to its preeminent position as county seat, established when Okanogan County was separated from Stevens County in 1888. When Matsura set down his black bag, bulky camera equipment, and tripod on the dusty streets of Conconully, he saw a collection of rough board shacks, some of them facing on boardwalks. They were the homes and stores, taverns and hotels that had survived the decline in the mining industry, the Depression of 1893, the flash flood of 1894 that sent a wall of water twelve feet deep through the streets, and a fire in 1901 that burned forests to the very edge of town. Matsura was dressed immaculately and formally in a suit, tie, white shirt, and hat. He seemed to be a man of culture and education, speaking English with scarcely an accent.

Having been hired from Seattle by Jess Dillabough, owner of the Hotel Elliott, as cook's helper and laundryman, he appeared to be an unlikely person for the job. But he moved into a small room behind the kitchen at the Elliott and attacked his duties with energy and cheerfulness. At first he was reserved and diffident, uncertain of his reception as the only Japanese in town. As his kind acts and natural sense of humor surfaced, he became a favorite with customers and staff, friendly, but always showing the deference required of a person in his menial position at the hotel.

Whenever he was off duty, he took pictures. With his head buried under a black cloth while he peered through the lens of his big camera on its tripod, Matsura was present at every important occasion in Conconully—picnics, birthday parties, Sunday School programs, and Teachers' Institute graduations.

At night after work Frank developed his photographs in the laundry-room sinks. Dorothy Mitchell, daughter of Frank Putnam of the *Okanogan Record,* Conconully's newspaper, recalled that when she was a child, Matsura permitted her and her friends to watch him develop pictures, "as long as we sat still and didn't talk too much." The Elliott Hotel had running water only in the kitchen, where creek water was piped to a spigot. From there water was carried next door to the laundry room. A critical element in processing film and paper, the creek water was unfiltered and ice-cold. Despite the unfavorable conditions, Matsura's work was good from the beginning and steadily improved. Intermittent notes in the *Okanogan Record* show the increasing respect of the community for his work (author's italics):

> June 17, 1904:
> Frank, the Japanese photographer, *is much in evidence* these days with his camera, taking views of the surrounding scenery.

> July 1, 1904:
> We have on our desk a panoramic view of Conconully, the compliments of Mr. Frank Matsura, which is a very creditable piece of work. Frank is *one of the most successful amateur photographers* in this section.

> A year and a half later on January 5, 1906:
> Frank Matsura who is one of the *best photographists* in this part of the country recently received a new camera....

> By March 15, 1907, the newspaper now reports:
> *Artist* Matsura returned from...

About a year after his arrival in Conconully, Matsura advertised one of his cameras, a large professional Kodak, in a classified ad in the *Okanogan Record* of July 22, 1904:

> No. 4 Eastman cartridge kodak either film or plate 4 x 5 inches with tripod, carrying case, plate holders, etc. $20. Inquire of Frank Matsuura, Elliott Hotel.

Sometimes he gave surplus cameras to his friends, according to Lillian Kaufman of Omak—and by now he had many friends. Basically an extrovert, Matsura attended local dances and parties and was popular with everyone.

Yet he divulged little about his past to anyone. Until research in Tokyo in 1981 uncovered a passport application made in 1901 by a Sakae Matsuura (Matsura's earliest photos were signed *Frank S. Matsuura*), residents of Okanogan believed him to be seven years younger than he was. The document shows his age as twenty-seven and states that he was "master of the family"; he may have been married. No one knew why he came to America or what his profession had been before he came. Years later, acquaintances thought he had been in the Japanese Army as an entertainer for the troops, a pantomime artist. Others said he was a newspaperman.

When the Russian-Japanese hostilities broke out in 1903, culminating in a full-scale war in 1904, Conconully's sympathies lay with Japan — quite possibly because of the townspeople's regard for Matsura, the only Japanese many of them had ever known. The *Okanogan Record*, a backwoods newspaper far from the international mainstream, devoted an inordinate amount of news coverage to the war, and Matsura was often asked to speak about it at social meetings. As part of his presentation, he sometimes performed a ceremonial dance, wearing a ceremonial sword. Such swords were a mark of the *samurai*, a high social class in Japan. *Samurai* included the imperial warriors, the feudal lords (called *daimios*), and the *shogun* himself, a total of about 5 percent of the Japanese population. Although the abolition of feudalism in 1871 stripped the *samurai* of their special privileges, families cherished their *samurai* ancestors.

According to an article about Matsura written by O. H. Woody in 1944 for the *Okanogan Independent,* Frank Matsura was summoned back to Japan for military service in 1904. He promptly packed his bags, said goodbye to his friends, and left for Seattle. Within two weeks he returned. Surprised to see him so soon, his friends greeted him jovially with, "Hey, Frank, have you won the war already?" He replied in the same vein: "I missed the boat!" More seriously, he told his friends that he arrived in Seattle, ready to board a ship for Japan, then asked himself why he should return when he had adopted America as his home. He resumed his job at the Elliott Hotel.

Not having a proper studio, Matsura took his photographs outdoors. He used both nitrate film and dry plates. The turn of the century was an evolutionary time for photographic processes. Since 1839, when the first photographic portrait was produced, photographers of the Indian wars and the Civil War had been burdened with the cumbersome and elaborate paraphernalia required for wet-plate processing — a dark-room tent, chemicals, and glass plates. The wet process entailed coating a piece of glass with a photosensitive solution, then exposing it while it was still wet. Since the plates had low photosensitivity, to get a clear picture, a person had to hold a pose for several minutes, which explains the frozen appearance of subjects in nineteenth-century prints. The image on an exposed wet plate had an average life of only two weeks, so after prints were made, the glass pieces were cleaned and reused.

In 1871, Dr. R. L. Maddox of England experimented with gelatin in the coating of plates. This stabilized the solution so that the glass remained photosensitive when dry. After 1880, dry plates were produced by George Eastman, but, because they were not reusable — and were therefore more expensive — many photographers continued to struggle with the wet plates. By Matsura's time, dry plates, reduced in cost by mass production, had largely replaced wet plates. Film research continued, too.

As early as 1888, Eastman produced the first Kodak, a hand-held camera only 6¾ inches by 3¾ inches, using flexible film to take pictures 2½ inches wide. Cost of the camera and a roll of film sufficient for 100 exposures was only $25. The drawback was that the purchaser had to send both camera and film to the Eastman laboratory in Rochester, New York, for processing and reloading as soon as the original 100 exposures were made. When wrapped or backed film was manufactured in 1895, facilitating daylight loading of cameras, the use of both dry and wet glass plates declined.

With improvements in photographic technology, more newspapers used photo-illustrations, but since the technique of printing photographs was too advanced for the *Okanogan Record,* Matsura's pictures did not find a market there. Nevertheless, he gravitated to the newspaper office, becoming friendly with the *Record's* editor, O. H. Woody, and Frank Putnam, a later owner. On March 31, 1905, the *Okanogan Record* published an article by Frank S. Matssura [*sic*] entitled "Education of Japanese Women." This literate piece of journalism started on a philosophical note:

> The great scholar, John Stuart Mill, has truly observed that the work of a state, in the long run, is the work of the individuals composing it. Equally so, do the vigor and strength of the nation solely depend upon the individual character of its members. From it emanate all the actions and deeds of industry, bravery and patriotism, and in it rest all the qualities essential for the advance of a nation, whether in peace or in war. A man's character is formed and moulded when he is young, nay, principally while at home under the care of his parents. Home education is the ground-work; no man can escape without more or less of its influence and this is the predominent [*sic*] work of the mothers. "The future destiny of the child is the work of the mother," said Napoleon.

Later in the article Matsura observed:

> The oldest Japanese records invariably record that women were regarded as equal to men in every respect.... They armed themselves like warriors and stood at the head of armies for their lords, fought battles and led invasions.... Every wife carried a dagger concealed in her bosom, not only to attack her enemy, but rather to kill herself on emergency when there was no escape from dishonor.

Dorothy Putnam Mitchell recalled that Matsura himself was very respectful of women and concerned about her mother and baby brother.

"He went to Japan once," she said, "intending to bring back a wife, I think, but he came back alone. He brought a beautiful scarf to my mother, instructing her to place it over baby Stanley's face during the cold weather."

Periodically, he went to Seattle, presumably to purchase supplies. Mitchell asserted than an aunt regularly sent money to Frank. In January 1906, he bought a new camera for $315, a very expensive camera indeed. To expand his income from photography, while still working part time at the Elliott Hotel, Matsura conceived the idea of making postcards out of his scenic photos. Suggesting that they would make good Christmas gifts, he advertised five different views, which were still, no doubt, being printed after work in the galvanized tubs of the Hotel Elliott.

Although postcards were first invented in 1869 by Dr. E. Hermann of Vienna, the first picture postcard is credited to a French stationer who published one during the Franco-German War in about 1894, commemorating the visit of a popular regiment to his city. In the Okanogan country, only twelve years later, Matsura introduced picture postcards to the Northwest frontier. He signed most of his work—postcards and prints—either *Frank S. Matsura* (he had dropped one *u* from his name) or *F.S.M.*

Not until he moved to Okanogan in 1907, when that town first was incorporated, did Matsura establish himself as a full-time photographer. Across First Avenue from Davidson & Richards General Store he built a crude two-room shack, equipping the back room as a darkroom and using the front room as a reception room and studio. He built a skylight into the roof, and Moses George, a local Indian leader and retired civil engineer, remembers seeing Matsura up on the roof on winter days, brushing the snow off the glass.

At this same time William Compton Brown, a young lawyer who eventually became a Superior Court judge, set up his practice in Okanogan. He and Matsura became close friends. In an article for the *Okanogan Independent* on January 7, 1954, Judge Brown recalled that on a May 1907 afternoon he and Matsura climbed a hill on the town's west side, and that he stood by while Matsura snapped the first panoramic photographs ever taken of Okanogan, a "historic moment." The friendship was to last beyond Matsura's untimely death, for Judge Brown stored three or four boxes of Matsura's plates and films, all that remained after Matsura's studio equipment was sold to pay funeral expenses, with the intention of opening them "twenty years in the future" to evaluate their historic significance. Involved in his legal practice and absorbed in research into Indian treaties that led to publication of his book, *The Indian Side of the Story*, Brown did not open the boxes until 1954, forty-one years after Matsura's death.

Brown's article paid tribute to Matsura:

> Smiling Frank S. Matsura brought his wit, a style for winning friends and a brilliant talent for photography to the Okanogan from Japan... he worked day and night, conducting his business with the finest of cameras and equipment.

In the style of the times, Frank was circumspect in his relationships with women. Dora Storhow Meeker, who once lived across the street from Matsura, said that when she or any other girl came to his studio, he would not permit her to enter, but would say, "Go home and get your sister [or your mother or friend] and we'll have tea." When she returned with a chaperone, Frank produced an elegant tea set from his back room, poured delicious tea, and served cookies.

At the time of its founding, Okanogan certainly had few such amenities as fine tea services. It was little more than a stage stop and — during high water, when the Columbia riverboats could navigate the Okanogan River — a port. Even so, until the advent of the railroad in 1913, the river provided the most practical access to the area. At Wenatchee one boarded the steamers, considered luxurious, with carpeted passenger areas and even a few staterooms.

Ascending the swift Columbia River was not easy; it had stretches of rapids and — at low water — boulders and snags. Above the worst white-water areas the Army Corps of Engineers installed large iron ringbolts on the rocks. Crews attached to the rings long lines with which they winched themselves up the river. At other, less vicious but still swift stretches, a line went ashore from the boat to waiting teams of horses that pulled the craft along. Because going downriver was treacherous, too, with unseen eddies waiting to toss a boat against the rocks, a crew sometimes attached lines to the ringbolts to "pay" themselves downriver.

The riverboats were endowed with the same aura of romance attached to the Mississippi riverboats of years past. Children knew all the boats and captains, rushed to the dock when a whistle signaled an imminent arrival, and dreamed of the day when they would stand at the helm of a riverboat.

Out of the sagebrush and sand along the river, Okanogan's handful of stores, taverns, livery stables, and hotels served the growing stream of homesteaders and ranchers who settled in the fertile valleys and on the benchlands. The alternately dusty and muddy streets were traveled equally often by Indians from adjacent lands. Cattle drives through town were common, and wild horses roamed the streets snatching hay from their tame brothers if they could. Loose horses periodically were rounded up by the local sheriff and his men; unless ranchers came to claim their renegade animals, establishing ownership from brands, the horses were sold at auction or shot.

During his first few months in Okanogan, Matsura photographed every aspect of the rough new town and its life — the boats, the schoolchildren, the construction of the U.S. Irrigation Project dam at Conconully, and the big ditches that led away to irrigate

Okanogan and Pogue Flat orchards. He made pictures of the verdant new apple, peach, and apricot orchards, the stages that came winter and summer from Brewster to Riverside and Conconully, the taverns, the drunks, and the Fourth of July parades. Many of his photographs appeared in the *Okanogan Independent,* founded by the same O. H. Woody who had formerly owned the *Okanogan Record* in Conconully and also owned the *Molson Independent.*

Matsura rented livery hacks and went out to photograph St. Mary's Mission, the Catholic school and hospital near Omak Lake; scenic spots around the county; and the ranches. He particularly liked to photograph the cowboys at work or in their Sunday best.

After cattle and horses were brought to the Okanogan by such people as "Okanogan" Smith, cattlemen Phelps and Wadleigh, and Dr. Joseph Pogue, ranching developed swiftly. The big ranches hired both Indian and white cowboys. Isolated from the influence of the big Texas and Oklahoma ranching empires, Northwest cowboys developed their own unique dress, horse tack, and ways of operating the cattle ranches. There were no ten-gallon hats, no flared leather chaps, no low-slung six-shooters, and few gunfighters, although there were a few notorious outlaws. Only if a man felt he qualified as a competent cowboy, did he don the "uniform" of angora chaps, dyed in brilliant colors—yellow, blue, red, green—a straight-brimmed hat similar to that of a cavalryman, straight English-style boots reaching almost to the knee, gloves or gauntlets with fancy beading, a neckerchief, and a vest. For rough work like branding, he wore leather chaps. A greenhorn did not dare to dress like a true cowboy for fear of being laughed at; the clothes became the mark of the professional.

The horses they rode were a conglomeration of interbred range animals, many captured from wild horse bands. The Nez Perce Indians, traditionally gamblers on horse races, had bred selectively the spotted horse known as the Appaloosa, and it was said that a cowboy would gladly swap his woman for "a Palousey horse." Flung over the backs of the rough-looking but sturdy horses was a form-fitting saddle that had a high cantle which dug into a man's back, and a high pommel topped by a vicious steel saddle horn. True, it was a saddle hard to fall out of, but if a horse fell, it was a man-killer. Saddles were single-rigged, that is, had one cinch; until the occasional Texas cowboy drifted up to the Northwest cattle country, double-rigged saddles were a curiosity. If he was riding a young or half-broke horse, the cowboy used a double-ring snaffle bit, running a loop over the horse's nose and through its legs to the cinch, to prevent the animal from rearing or throwing himself and the rider over backwards.

The cowboy's lariat was his individual creation. A favorite pattern was variegated colors of cowhide cut into strips and braided. After braiding, the lariat was boiled in lard to make it supple, then kept soft by regular applications of beef tallow. Horsehair ropes were popular because hair was readily available and the long strands, when braided, were very strong.

Despite the large number of photographs of Okanogan life Matsura offered for sale, sales in 1908 were very low. There was, after all, an average of only one person per square mile in the entire county. By late February 1908, Matsura had doubts about his ability to survive solely on photography and placed an ad in the local paper:

WANTED: A Japanese wants a position as cook.

A job did not materialize. Within a week or two he received money from a benefactor—perhaps it was the aunt in Seattle, as Mitchell believed, or a cousin in New York, as others said. Instead of advertising further for a cook's job, he bought a

18

stamp-photo camera, a large portrait camera, a backdrop, and other equipment required for studio work.

The stamp-photo machine was a special camera with a battery of small lenses partitioned into as many frames as there were lenses. The photographer snapped one view, moved a portion of the dark slide protecting the photosensitive plate to expose a new frame, took a new view, and so on. Thus, Matsura got as many as twelve views on one plate. Printed in the actual size of the image on the plate, the small photos were a fad of the time, inexpensive enough for friendly exchange. A true stamp effect was gained by perforating the edges with a special machine after the backs of the photos had been brushed with dextrine, an adhesive, and allowed to dry.

A friend of the neighborhood children, Matsura often photographed them and gave them a free stamp photo or two. His own cohorts found the stamp-photo camera a source of great entertainment, clowning around in Matsura's studio in costumes, making faces, and staging pictures. Matsura himself took hilarious self-portraits, exhibiting a wide range of facial expressions and even dressing up in Indian blankets, clown costumes, and baby bonnets.

His more serious work was beginning to gain recognition outside of Okanogan County. The Okanogan Commercial Club had photos of orchards and ranches run in Eastern publications to tout the charms of the Okanogan region for homesteading. Matsura traveled to Spokane to photograph the prize-winning entries of Okanogan County in the apple expositions, the pictures later appearing in the *Okanogan Independent*. In 1907 a commission was formed in Seattle, made up of representatives from all over Washington State, to organize an Alaska-Yukon-Pacific Exposition to be held in 1909 to commemorate the tenth anniversary of the arrival of the first ship bearing Klondike gold. Washington counties were asked to send displays and photographs of industries, resources, and scenery. When J. A. McCormick, official photographer for AYP, received Matsura's photographs of Okanogan County, he sent a letter to him stating that, while he was receiving views from the entire state — indeed from all over the nation — Matsura's collection of photographs was the best he had secured. The Alaska-Yukon-Pacific Exposition ran all summer in Seattle, attracting notables such as William Jennings Bryan, President Taft, and Henry Ford. After the fair was over, the 154 photographs that had been exhibited were distributed among the various state offices — Matsura's scenes undoubtedly among them.

On October 27, 1911, Robert Mills, the advertising manager of Great Northern Railway Company, came to Okanogan to select about forty of Matsura's photos of the Okanogan Valley to be used in publicizing the Okanogan. The Great Northern encouraged settlement because it was extending its rail lines northward from Wenatchee, and more people meant more revenue. The photos were exhibited nationally, along with displays of North Central Washington apples, at state and county fairs and on roving promotional trains.

An advertisement outlining Matsura's abilities ran in the *Okanogan Independent* for years:

PHOTOGRAPHER
FRANK MATSURA
Stamp Photos Taken   Souvenir Postcards   Developing Plates and Films
PRINTING DONE FROM NEGATIVES
Special Attention to Portrait and Scenic Photography

Prices Are Reasonable
Work Promptly Done
Gallery on 1st Avenue   Okanogan, Washington

His portrait business thrived. It was popular not only among the townspeople but also among the young cowboys and Indians, who came to town dressed in their best finery for formal photographs. Through his trips to the Colville lands to photograph the scenery and Indian life, and because of his association with Bill Muldrow, surveyor of the South Half of the Colville lands, Matsura had developed good rapport with the Indian people. Moses George said that Matsura and he were amused by the mutual difficulty of the Japanese and the Indians in pronouncing the letter L. A story also told about Matsura is that strangers who came to town sometimes addressed him in pidgin English. Straight-faced, Matsura would lapse into an outrageous flood of broken English. If the stranger stayed long enough, he learned to his dismay that Matsura — except for a slight accent — spoke flawlessly.

Although gradually adopting the white man's ways of raising cattle and crops, most of the Indians on the Colville lands still lived in tepees, particularly in the summer. They retained their medicine men and women and danced their secret Chinook dances to influence the coming of a good spring or bring the salmon up the river. Of the diverse bands of Indians on the sprawling Colville lands, some — the bands of Chief Joseph and Chief Moses — really did not belong there.

After the historic flight of Chief Joseph and his Nez Perce from the Wallowa Mountains to Montana, and their surrender because of hunger, the chief and some of his band were sent first to Oklahoma, then to the Colville land near Nespelem. Bitter and aging, Chief Joseph squabbled with the Indians native to those lands and with Chief Moses, another outsider cast into their midst. Powerful and known nationwide because he had been to Washington, D.C. for consultations with presidents, Chief Moses, the head of the *Sin-ka-yoush,* or Half Sun People, originally had rights to an area encompassing most of today's Douglas, Grant, and Kittitas counties, the Wenatchee Valley, and the Entiat area of Chelan. Because of errors and misunderstandings during negotiations with the U.S. Government, Moses and his band were not assigned any specific land in the Indian Treaty of 1855. In 1879, they were given a legal refuge on the west side of the Columbia and Okanogan rivers, but in 1886, because few had moved to the refuge, they were removed to Colville lands permanently, though not welcomed by their native brothers.

In Matsura's time these diverse bands with various heritages were trying to live peacefully and adapt to new ways, knowing that they had no other choice. With common aims of survival in the remote Okanogan land, and sharing lifestyles that were similar (ranching, fishing, hunting, building crude homes), the Indians and settlers intermarried frequently and mingled freely in the celebrations of the time — the Fourth of July celebrations, the parades, and the horse races that marked holidays or were sponsored by Okanogan and Omak merchants to encourage business.

Added to Matsura's gallery in 1909 were some Oriental curios that he had purchased in Seattle. During the Christmas rush, business was so brisk that he hired two assistants. He became prosperous enough to purchase two lots on Second Avenue in Okanogan, moving from his room at the back of a store to a small house on his newly acquired property. During the long, warm summer evenings he planted and tended masses of flowers around his house. Whenever a friend became ill, Matsura sent from this immense garden a bouquet of flowers delivered by one of the many children who played there. Among the flowers he installed a set of parallel bars and two huge swings for the youngsters.

Matsura sometimes mentioned to his friends that he thought he had tuberculosis and would not live long, but, as he seemed so energetic and frequently joked, few took him seriously. To his friend at the newspaper, O. H. Woody, he once said, "I have to die. I'm glad I'm a Christian. I can't live long." Among Matsura's prints was found a letter from Japan addressed to Sakae and written by a woman named Noriko, whose relationship to Matsura is unknown. She hoped that he was "recovering his health." After his death in 1913, friends remembered that early in 1912 he had contracted a severe cold, which seemed to hang on and on.

In October 1912, Matsura announced that his gallery would be closed indefinitely because of ill health. That illness was fairly brief; at Christmas he again advertised his stock of novelties, postcards, and Japanese curios, and in February 1913, he added facilities for framing pictures.

Within the month he was in severe pain. In its later stages, tuberculosis produces symptoms similar to arthritis. In the *Okanogan Independent* of February 21, 1913, Matsura advertised:

> Owing to trouble with rheumatism and being unable to attend to the store end of my business, I have decided to sell my showcases, about 10,000 postcards, 2 tower postcard racks, cash register, typewriter, oriental curios, silks, pictures, etc., and devote my time to my photographic work and picture framing. Call and see the goods. FRANK MATSURA.

Despite increasing pain, Matsura continued to roam through Okanogan County that spring, taking pictures of the railroad crews as they laid rails to Okanogan and Omak, and the orchards spreading throughout the Okanogan Valley, the result of the Irrigation Project. Always there were photos of the daily life of homesteaders and Indians, whose numbers had increased, according to the 1910 census, to 12,561 living in the 5,221 square miles of Okanogan County. Frequently he rode into the countryside with Bill Muldrow, the surveyor, who had become one of his closest friends.

It was to Muldrow he turned the night of his death, June 16, 1913. During a routine patrol the city marshal, Joe Leader, noticed a window open in Neumann's Store and went to investigate. Stopping the first passerby, who happened to be Frank Matsura, Leader asked him to fetch Mr. Neumann so he could determine if anything was missing. Matsura set out at a run for Neumann's house. Just as he arrived, he was taken with a fit of coughing. Alarmed and fighting for breath, he changed direction, ran across the street and up the steps of Bill Muldrow's house, and began to beat on the door. The startled Mrs. Muldrow screamed out in fright, and her house guests, Mr. and Mrs. Dick Everett, rushed out to see what was the matter. They found Frank Matsura lying on the lawn, coughing up blood, and choking. Everett ran for the doctor but couldn't find him, and when he returned, Matsura was dead.

Shocked neighbors carried the body off to undertaker McCampbell and queried the Japanese consul in Tacoma, requesting instructions for notification of relatives and disposition of Matsura's body. When the consul replied that there was no information available, that Okanogan residents should bury him where he was, the citizens gave Matsura the largest funeral held in the town to that time; there was standing room only at the auditorium.

The *Okanogan Independent* of June 20, 1913, reported:

> A shadow of sorrow was cast over the community early in the week by the sudden death on Monday night of Frank S. Matsura, the Japanese photographer who has been a part and parcel of the city ever since its establishment seven years ago.... Although an unpretentious, unassuming, modest little Japanese, Frank Matsura's place in Okanogan city will never be filled. He was a photographer of fine ability and his studio contains a collection of views that form a most complete photographic history of this city and surrounding country, covering a period of seven or eight years. He was always on the job. Whenever anything happened Frank was there with his camera to record the event.... He has done more to advertise Okanogan city and valley than any other individual.

Furthermore Frank Matsura was a gentleman in every sense of the word. He held the highest esteem of all who knew him. He was one of the most popular men in Okanogan, and was known from one end of this vast county to the other. . . . He was well educated, being a graduate from a Japanese college at Tokio, and had done newspaper work in his native land. He came from a wealthy and aristocratic family in Japan.

Frank Matsura's grave in the Masonic Cemetery of Okanogan is on a benchland overlooking the long valley and the ragged brown hills of the Colville Indian lands. The white-capped North Cascades Mountains loom in the distance. It's a simple resting place among his old friends, a grave tended throughout the years first by Judge William Compton Brown and later by Addie Mitchell of the Okanogan County Historical Society, a pioneer herself. Enlargements by John Andrist of some of Matsura's photographs are displayed prominently in the small town's museum, to make the Okanogan country's history come alive. The lively spirit of Frank S. Matsura — or Sakae Matsuura, if that's who he was — lives on in his photographs, windows on the Okanogan frontier.

Chelsea Woodward was a surveyor for the U. S. Coast & Geodetic Survey and for the County of Okanogan. He was an avid hunter and fisherman.

Whitestone Mountain west of Tonasket.

Rattlesnake Point near Ophir, a junction of the Brewster-Okanogan wagon road and the railroad.

Duley Lake was southeast of Okanogan in an otherwise stark, dry rangeland.

The Duley Ranch on the South Half of the Colville lands was one of the largest spreads in northern Washington. Cattle ran wild until marketing, looked after by the cowboys.

Tug of war on horseback was a popular sport. On the ranch a roping horse learned to drag a roped calf near the fire, even after its rider left the saddle to do the branding. The horse had to tolerate the calf's resistance, kicking and pulling away.

Cowboys "stretch out" a calf, letting the horses do all the work; otherwise one man would have had to sit on the calf's head and shoulders while another branded, castrated and earmarked the animal. Calves were branded as early as possible because a calf running "slick" might be "borrowed" by a rustler.

Ranchers swam their cattle across the Okanogan River to pick up the trail southward. Before the railroad came, ranchers herded cattle in big drives through Naches Pass or Snoqualmie Pass into Seattle's livestock yards.

The Yakima Cattle Company, headed by one-time mayor of Yakima A. J. Splawn, bought cattle all over the North Cascades, using their own crews to drive them to markets.

Indian cowboys on the banks of the Okanogan River. From left to right: Paul Timentwa, Joe Louie, Joe Thomas, Pierce McCragie, Paul Antoine, Sam Samuels — all Colville Indians. Ranchers impartially hired the best men, Indians and whites, for their vast cattle operations.

Rough Riders.

FRANK MATSURA PHOTO.

Madison Winfield "Matt" Duley, standing center, was the first rancher to raise hay, moving his cattle from the Duley Lake summer range to the Okanogan River valley hayfields for wintering.

Marc Thomas, Sheriff of Okanogan County for a time; Sam Michel George, and two other cowboys.

Johnny Poynton, medicine man and rancher, and friend, Marc Thomas. Thomas and his friends had a hunter's cabin north of Okanogan. When all had retired, Thomas sometimes extinguished the candles by shooting them out.

Johnny Poynton and Johnny Innis, Colville cowboys and ranchers. Poynton became a medicine man in later years, a "blue jay." As such, he could sing and whistle like a blue jay and, during the secret Chinook dances, could go through a window into the outside world, returning in two or three days to tell of things that he saw, spiritual things.

The Cowboy and the City Dude. The style of dress indicates that the pair were Canadians.

Ambrose, a Colville cowboy. His winter-thin horse is shod, somewhat unusual for the early 1900s. Cattle and horses seldom were fed hay, shifting for themselves in winter by pawing through snow to reach dried grass.

Johnnie Louie and an unidentified Federal officer. Louie, a Colville Indian from the Aeneas Valley, was an interpreter who went to Washington, D.C. with the chiefs when discussion was required, especially during the sales of portions of the Colville lands.

A cowboy named Barrett and Paul "Long Paul" Timentwa. Timentwa was a Colville rancher.

Michel Charlie, a Methow Indian from Malott, in his bulky winter coat, and C. B. Suszen Timentwa, who became chief of the Kartar Valley band in 1930.

The Okanogan-Nespelem stage ran on an erratic schedule, its departures depending on demand.

Tepees were cool in summer, easily moved.

As long as anyone can remember, Indians have gathered at Nespelem for socializing. It was a place for barbecues, horse races, stick and bone games, telling the old stories.

The Blessing

Sam George of Okanogan and his large family.

Minnie McDonald was known to like fine horses. She wound up in jail for horse theft.

Kanum-tith, Captain Jim, and his wife *Ha-mauh,* or Mary. Born in 1805, Captain Jim was a scout for the U. S. Government and, upon his death, was given a military funeral. Captain Jim and Mary lived in an old house or dugout in Okanogan during their last years. A dignified old man, he liked to reminisce about his military service and often wore his uniform with brass buttons.

FUNERAL PROCESSION OF CAPT. JIM, AN OLD INDIAN. T.S.K.

During the last days of Captain Jim and Mary, citizens of Okanogan cared for them—especially W. R. Kahlow, a crusty old Prussian who watched over them, notified the Government officials when Captain Jim died, and saw to it that he received proper honors. The Storhow family brought a hot meal each day to his widow until she passed on.

Wild West outlaws were rare in the Okanogan, but Johnny McLain had a reputation as a mean one. Indians and whites alike were afraid of him. Once he opened the gates of a corral containing wild horses that cowboys had spent all day rounding up. A resentful cowboy shot him, but not fatally. Later McLain was convicted of killing a rancher named Cameron.

Black bears commonly roamed the Okanogan country. Pioneers often fashioned their pelts into winter coats that reached from ankles to ears.

Peter Reilly's cabin. In 1889 it was the only cabin between Malott and Okanogan.

Koxit George, or William George, a Chief of the Moses band in 1910, at St. Mary's Mission near Omak Lake. In 1887, the famed *Que-tal-a-kin,* or Chief Moses, met with his other chiefs on the shores of Omak Creek to decide whether the missionaries would be allowed to remain. When a child who fell into the water was rescued by a priest, the Indians decided they could stay. Out of crude beginnings came a school and hospital. In 1906, 143 Indian and 3 white boys attended; in 1907-8, 50 girls also came. The priests taught Latin and Greek; the students read Caesar and Horace and learned math up to trigonometry.

In 1912, elegantly tailored riding skirts and jackets were the vogue.

WOMAN AND MAN TRAVELLING THROUGH WESTERN COUNTRY.
PHOTO BY FRANS MATSURA. #385

Both man and woman are mounted on Appaloosa horses, a colorful breed much favored by the Colville, Nez Perce, Okanogan and Palouse Indians for their stamina, speed and gentle disposition. "Appaloosa" grew out of the term "a Palouse" horse.

A windmill on Pogue Flat brought water to the summer-parched orchards. Apple and plum trees were first introduced by Dr. Joseph I. Pogue, an Eastern doctor who moved west seeking adventure. He made little money at medicine, raising horses and fruit for his living.

A complex pole structure for stacking alfalfa hay at Grant Elgin's ranch, south of Shellrock Point between Omak and Okanogan.

Horse-drawn combines utilized as many as thirty-two horses, but this hitch had eighteen. The combine's header or cutter sheared off the grain, which went up a chute through the machine for threshing. The straw went out the back and the grain through the side into a "doghouse," where an attendant sacked it.

Will Daniel of Spring Coulee grew wheat that was over six feet four inches tall without irrigation. Still, the crop was not as profitable as apples, so wheat farming was confined largely to the lands east of the Columbia River.

Before the advent of the railroad, sacked grain was loaded onto riverboats for transport to city markets. Wagons and teams streamed to and from the docks during harvest time.

Ostenberg Creamery at Spring Coulee, where milk was dumped and local news exchanged.

Pleasant Valley between Okanogan and Loup Loup.

Omak in 1911.

At the docks of Okanogan are the *Enterprise* (129 tons, 86 feet, built 1903) and the *North Star* (144 tons, 100 feet, built 1902). Fire destroyed the *North Star* in 1915, along with two other riverboats. The same year, the *Enterprise* foundered in rough Columbia River waters near Brewster.

The *Okanogan* (432 tons, 137 feet, built 1907). It was destroyed by fire with the *North Star* at port in Wenatchee. The riverboats were considered luxurious, with carpeted passenger areas, even a few staterooms. To navigate the worst areas of the Columbia, crews fixed long lines to large ringbolts on rocks ashore, winching themselves upriver.

Steel bridge at Pateros.

The *North Star* at Brewster. Riverboats ran about once weekly for horses, cows, people, apples, wheat, prospectors' machinery, lumber.

Conconully Lake was a popular fishing spot. It was divided by a spit into two sections and connected by a small stream.

The Okanogan Government Irrigation Project derived its water from Salmon Creek, which had a heavily timbered watershed. Several saw mills operated within fifteen miles of Conconully to provide the lumber needed for dam frameworks and flumes.

The Okanogan Irrigation Project at Conconully was one of the first projects implemented by the U. S. Reclamation Act. The first dam built at Conconully did not hold water and the designer was replaced. By 1910, the Conconully Dam was completed.

The main canal of the Okanogan Irrigation Project through Pogue Flat.

Fruit orchards south of Malott along the Okanogan River.

Apricot orchard three years old, owned by Frank Garber.

J. S. White cabin and orchard. Cabins were made of rough lumber chinked with a mixture of mud and hair.

During the early 1900s the Spokane National Apple Show drew entries from fruit-growing counties. In 1909, Okanogan County won ten firsts and four seconds, including a prize for the largest perfect apple: a Wolf River apple, weighing 25 ounces and measuring 16⅝ inches in circumference. Other varieties winning were: Rhode Island Greening, Northwest Greening, Yellow Bellflower, Yellow Newton.

Omak Fruit Growers membership had an annual meeting and picnic on board the *Okanogan*.

Installing the waterworks at Omak in 1910 was a pick-and-shovel task. Water was supplied from the Okanogan River to the downtown area only.

DAMPING DIRT BY SWANSON BROS OF G.N.R.R. AT OKANOGAN.
F.S.M.

Swanson Bros., one of the contractors building roadbed for the Great Northern Railway Company, used horse-drawn Fresno scrapers.

PETERSON'S CREW, G.N.R.R. OKANOGAN LINE. LAST FINISH. FRANK MATSURA PHOTO

Peterson's track-laying crew, one of several laying rails northward from Wenatchee.

In 1910 a delegation from the Great Northern Railway Company was greeted by Harry Kerr, a local banker, at Okanogan.

By April 1913, the Great Northern was operating to Riverside.

The *North Star* at Riverside, end of navigable water on the Okanogan River.

Twisp in 1909, a Methow Valley town connected to Okanogan by the Loup Loup trail.

The Ruby Mine near Conconully was discovered by John Clonan, Thomas Donan, William Mulligan and Thomas Fuller in 1886.

Most mines were small, one- or two-man operations. From 1886 to 1893, and again in the 1900s, there were many gold, silver and copper strikes along the eastern slope of the North Cascades. Only a few mines were successful.

Fish Lake, a top fishing spot between Conconully and Loomis.

Conconully was the first county seat when Okanogan County was officially separated from Stevens County in 1888. According to Alexander Ross, fur factor for the North West Company in 1814, it took its name from Con-con-ulps, the principal family of the *Oackinacken* Indian nation.

Located in the heart of mining activities, Conconully flourished from 1886 until 1914, when prospecting had declined and the town lost its designation as county seat to the town of Okanogan.

Street scene on a Sunday, Conconully, in the year 1908.

A birthday party at Conconully, 1906.

Adelbert M. Dewey (far right), the President of Q. S. Mining & Smelting Company, a copper mine property, hired surveyors in 1907 for a proposed Okanogan Electric Railway from Brewster through Conconully and Loomis to Nighthawk. There it was to intercept a proposed east-west route of the Great Northern. The group shown were working in the Sinlahekin Valley.

The bear was a pet of a Conconully resident, who raised it from a cub. One evening a saloonkeeper asked the man to bring it in as a curiosity, but refused to pay him anything. Later the disgruntled man released his bear into the saloon when it was full of patrons, quickly emptying the place.

Far from any large city, Okanogan created its own diversions. At left is Harry Stark, a sheriff of Okanogan County.

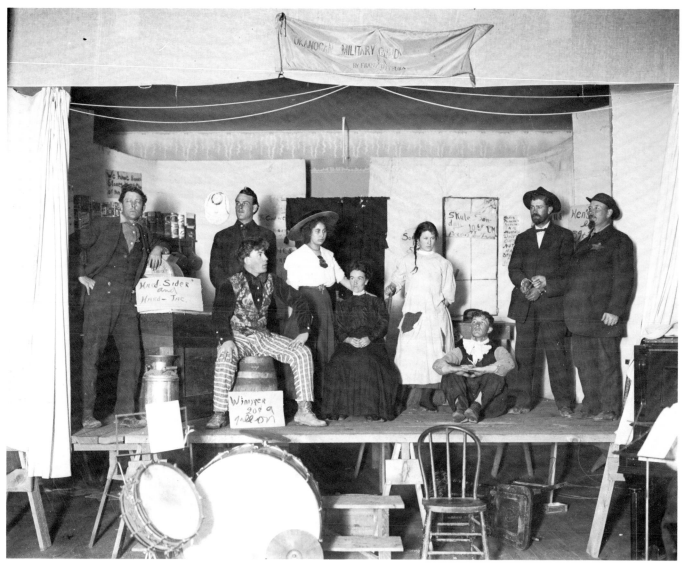

Home talent shows were highlights of each winter season.

Queen Edna Jones and her King at the Conconully Winter Carnival.

Boating on the Okanogan River in 1911 were Leona Schaller, a friend, Mathilda Schaller, and Leo Folkerson.

Whenever possible, a high school had a football team. Headgear consisted of any kind of padding a player could devise to protect himself. The Okanogan team of 1909 was coached by Professor Savage.

Football game at Okanogan.

TENNIS GAME, OKANOGAN, WASH.   F.S.M.

Tennis was a gentleman's sport. Competitors wore white shirts and straw hats. Okanogan's first tennis tournament, in 1911, drew entrants from Omak, Okanogan, Brewster, Pateros, Conconully, and the U. S. Reclamation Service.

Swimming in the Okanogan River, 1910.

The Okanogan River froze solid each winter, and one could skate for miles. Orril Gard and a friend, Mr. Hermann.

When the snow was deep, wagons were stored and sleighs used. Well-bred livery teams with fancy harness and bells were available at most Okanogan towns.

To preserve foods during the hot, dry summers, families needed to cut and store ice in winter. Packed in heavy straw or hay, the ice was placed in log bunkers, caves or dirt cellars.

Each winter the Storhows, commercial cutters, sawed ice in squares, storing it in an icehouse layered with sawdust, for summer deliveries to customers' iceboxes. The ferry was often icebound in winter.

The Okanogan River ferry, 1907.

The winter stage between Okanogan and Brewster.

Okanogan in the snow, February 11, 1909.

Riverboat *Columbia* at Pier No. 1, Okanogan. Empty grain sacks for the coming harvest are stacked on the dock.

Pier No. 1, Okanogan. Full grain sacks await transport.

The Okanogan Fire Brigade with Fire Chief L.H.C. Mintzer at right. The mascot is Fred Wilson's dog "Dixie." Whenever fire broke out, horses were seized from any livery stable to pull the equipment. One year Kahlow's livery itself caught fire, burning off the roof, but firemen saved the stabled horses by turning them loose. Fifty or sixty horses from various freight teams headed home, as much as one hundred miles distant. It took days to round them up again.

The fruit cannery at Okanogan was organized to can tomatoes but failed after only one year's operation.

In 1907 there were three saloons in Okanogan. Respectable women never went into them, and even glanced the other way while passing them. Indoor plumbing did not come to town until at least 1910; each business had its own privy.

Dad Harris Saloon, Okanogan.

On Sunday mornings the single men sat and talked at the street corner next to the pool hall. Matsura was one of the bachelors.

The stage from Brewster to Conconully. Passengers got off the Columbia River steamers at Brewster, boarded the stage at dawn and were off in dust or mud, the horses trotting or loping most of the time. The roads were rutted trails. At Malott the teams were changed, passengers fed. From Brewster to Okanogan took about eight hours. Teams were changed again at the Jones place on Salmon Creek and the stage arrived in Conconully by nightfall.

1911. Stage line serving Brewster, Malott, Conconully, Okanogan, Omak and Riverside.

The Brewster-Conconully-Riverside stage sets out from Okanogan.

A new Alco Auto Stage served the Okanogan Valley, 1913.

Second Avenue, Okanogan, 1908.

"I don't believe there is another community in the United States that can boast the development the Wenatchee Valley has made since the railroad was built there, but their advancement is little as compared with yours when we consider the disadvantages you have labored under. Now all you need is the magic of transportation... the state government will... help you acquire that one thing." Governor M. E. Hay, Okanogan, October 27, 1911, at the Auditorium.

Governor M. E. Hay. Okanogan. Wash.

FRANK MATSURA
PHOTO.

Dr. Warren Moore and his wife lived in rooms at the rear of the hospital, new in 1911. Mrs. Moore was a fine musician, popular with everyone in Okanogan.

The first automobile into Okanogan was a Locomobile driven by Ira Freese of Brewster. When he bought the car, Freese was able to start but could not stop; he drove around until it ran out of gas.

A party from the Wenatchee Community Club arrives at Okanogan after a ninety-five-mile drive over wagon roads.

On holidays and other special days merchants donated prizes for horse races. The racecourse was on the main street.

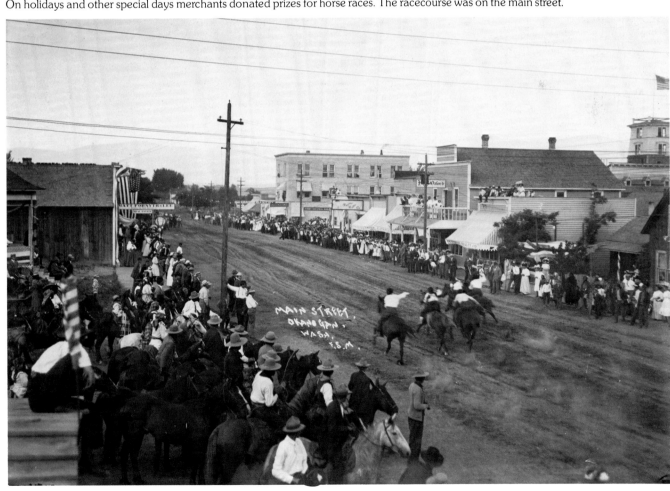

SPINNING ROPE BY INDIAN. OKANOGAN, WASH.

Cowboys still drove wild horses through the streets of town in 1912. Wild herds yielded free mounts, if one could catch and tame them. City dwellers found the herds a nuisance because they roamed through the settled areas. Periodically the sheriff's men rounded up all loose horses and sold them.

Street scene after the rain.

In front of the Bureau Hotel.

A group of Wenatchee and Chelan Indian women and children in town for a Fourth of July celebration. Left to right are Josephine Camille, unidentified boy, a Wapato son, Monique Simon, Julianne Loup Loup Dick, Martha Timentwa, unidentified girl.

1909 Fourth of July Parade.

Schaller's Bakery float in the Fourth of July Parade, 1910.

Traveling road shows or medicine shows were popular. Professor A. Kobe exhibited his strength as local men bent a steel rod around his neck. Later, a steel cable was attached to the three-story Bureau Hotel and stretched at a steep angle to the ground. Kobe slid down the cable by gripping with his teeth a small piece of leather affixed to a pulley.

On July 5, 1910, these two men still were celebrating.

Sam Shell George, a Wenatchee Indian, who died as a child. An Indian baby always was laced onto the board to be carried on its mother's back or hung from the saddle horn of her horse. The baby wore buckskin pants containing shredded cattails to absorb moisture.

An Indian boy who may have been part Chinese. There was considerable intermarriage between Chinese miners along the international border and Indians.

George and Louise Zacherle with their cousin, Frank Galler, at right. Their father, John Zacherle, was a German immigrant working as a cook at St. Mary's Mission. His wife, Pauline Cleveland, a Colville Indian, was a teacher there. Intermarriage between white settlers and Indians was common.

Lucie Nesom, a Chelan Indian.

Cecile Joe, Colville. Shells were obtained from the coastal Indians through trade missions that traveled over an arduous North Cascades mountain trail.

Chief Koxit George of the Moses band.

Moses George, son of Chief Koxit George, in his bear coat.

Kwa-ni, wife of Chief Koxit George. Buckskin shirts and skirts were tanned so finely that, according to New York merchants of 1900, commercial processes could not duplicate the softness of the handmade dress.

Paul Wapato, a Chelan Indian, was an evangelist in the Methow Valley and elsewhere.

La-ka-kin, Chilliwhist Jim. A Methow Indian from Malott. Respected as a prosperous rancher, he also was a medicine man of great power. His wife was Lucie Sheolum or *She-numtk.*

La-ka-kin, Chilliwhist Jim. The weasel skins hanging from his shoulder marked him as a man with spiritual power or a "medicine man." He never told anyone from whom he derived his power but, because he had an eagle headdress, it might be assumed that the eagle was his mentor. His pouch was a repository for tobacco, pipes, roots and herbs for medicine.

Wenatchee Indians. *Twit-mich,* also known a "Big Jim," Charley Leo, Suzanne Leo of his family (not wife), Suzanne's son Joe or "Little Joe." Charley Leo was a rancher. Suzanne Leo was a medicine woman or doctor.

Charley Leo and his wife.

Johnny Louie, an interpreter, and Matthew Bill, Chelan rancher.

Sam Michel, Mac Favel, George Haines, Francis Favel in front.

The Hold-Up.

W. R. Kahlow, who owned a livery stable and a hotel in Okanogan, was an imposing figure even at seventy-odd years. He was well over six feet tall and carried a long red bamboo staff. He was a declared and vociferous socialist.

Billy Collins at right, owner of a local men's clothing store, and other businessmen.

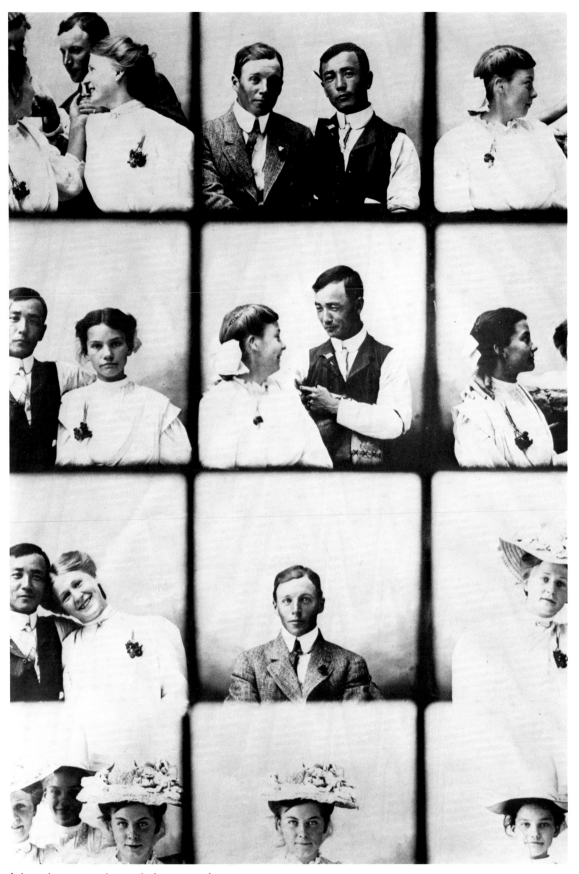

Informal portraits taken with the stamp photo camera.

Matsura's studio. He converted most of his photos into postcards offered for sale, even some of individuals photographed in his studio. Eventually he put in a retail section with Oriental curios and gifts.

Matsura's studio was located next to the stage stop, Davidson & Richards General Store. It was little more than a shack of two rooms. The building had a skylight in its roof, from which Matsura had to dust off the snow in winter by crawling up on the roof.

SOUVENIR POST CARDS
SEASON POST CARDS
VIEWS, POST CARD ALBUMS
DEVELOPING PLATES OR FILMS
PRINTING FROM NEGATIVES
PICTURE FRAMES MADE TO ORDER

PORTRAIT WORK
SCENIC VIEWS
STAMP PHOTOS TAKEN
PHOTOS ENLARGED
PHOTOS ON PILLOW TOPS

FRANK S. MATSURA

Photographer

OKANOGAN,

WASHINGTON